A Kudzu Vine of Blood and Bone

A Kudzu Vine of Blood and Bone

Poems

Tristan Tuttle

ISBN: 978-0-578-37697-4

Cover design by Get Covers

❀ Created with Vellum

For Jared, Jubilee, and Rejoice.
I love y'all. Stay wild and weird forever.

Author's Note

Dear Reader,

Please know that this collection addresses subjects like body image, suicide, anxiety, religion, and death. *A Kudzu Vine of Blood and Bone* is the story of my personal journey into motherhood, the natural world, and spirituality; these poems are a reflection of my experiences and are not expectations that I have for anyone else. Our lives are a gift, and I hope you will receive this glimpse into mine with grace and understanding.

All my love,
Tristan

THE MONSTER UNDER THE BED

They say, "Don't feed your fear,"
but I stay up late shoving blackened and charred
bits of
what ifs and *not enoughs*
into his cavernous mouth.

He's hungriest at night.

WHAT TO EXPECT WHEN YOU'RE EXPECTING

You cursed the ground and the serpent, but you
did not curse me.
There is merely a resistance.
The sins of the mother are not passed to the
daughter.
You did not set me apart for destruction.
Adam had to labor to bring forth life from the
ground, and I must labor to bring forth life as well.

No Place Like Home

I'm pregnant, sick, and desperate to be left
untouched by the child outside of my womb and
for the one inside to be still for just a few minutes.
What I want is quiet.

What I want is to go home.

Home is my mama's arms where she rocked and
prayed and loved me until I felt better.
I want to crawl up in her lap and let her tell me
that I will be okay and ask do I need anything else?
No, I would say.
This is enough.

NIGHT BIRTHS

Night birthed both my girls.

The first girl came in flashes of lightning--
Electricity crackling through my hips and back--
Days of weeping and wailing and gnashing of
teeth.
The next girl came in peaceful waves of darkness,
The occasional groan of discomfort and soft
laughter from the TV.
Night birthed both my girls, from darkness into
light.

Night birthed me into motherhood.

Screaming, writhing, searing pain turned into
blessed tranquility.
Me crying as the night deepened and my breasts
ached, and yet they couldn't satisfy the small
bundle in my arms.
The sickly-sweet smell of her burning skin under
the Bili lights filled the room.

Each night births a new day and each day a new
mother is born.
His mercies are new every morning
and so am I, as I am birthed into motherhood.

Postpartum Google Searches

- How much hair loss is too much hair loss?
- How much do plumbers charge to unclog drains?
- Spicy foods affect/effect breast milk?
- When to use affect or effect?
- How to hand express breast milk?
- Best formula to supplement with?
- Formula recall?!?
- Gentle parenting vs. spanking
- How to keep toddler from accidentally smothering infant sibling?
- Safe co-sleeping practices
- SIDS
- When will I stop accidentally peeing?
- Local pelvic floor rehab center
- Cost of professional pelvic floor rehab?
- At home pelvic floor exercises
- Why am I so angry postpartum?
- Postpartum depression
- Postpartum anxiety
- Postpartum rage
- How long can a person go without sleep?
- Is it safe to drive on no sleep?
- When do babies sleep through the night?
- Cry-it-out method
- Sleep training
- Momcations
- Best beaches in USA

- Airline tickets
- How to lose the baby weight?
- How to calm a crying baby?
- How to calm a crying mom?

My Body Is Gone

And it's up to me to get it back.
At least that's how it seems.
My mom friends on Facebook share tips and tricks
about shrinking my belly and tell me about a
special cream to rub on my thighs that will erase
the stretch marks.
As if I need to hide any and all evidence that
two baby girls traversed eternity to come earthside
through me.

My body is gone. Have you seen it?

Oh, wait. Here it is.

It's cushioning this baby girl while she coos at
me from my arms.
Earlier, it rocked a four-year-old and sang her to
sleep.
Just yesterday, it loved a man and sighed in
pleasure.
It's been here all along!

Is there a wrap to shrink the world's desire to
make me less?
A cream to eradicate the notion that mothers
need to bounce back from pregnancy like it wasn't
a nine+ month journey to get there?
A pill that will trick our collective brains into

seeing birth like a privilege and not a mess that
should be cleaned up as soon as it's over?
An essential oil distilled to its purest essence to
show us that pregnancy and birth are holy
experiences and the scars are proof we have
encountered the Sacred?

It turns out, my body is right where it is supposed
to be.

A Public Service Announcement

Cauliflower is not a substitute for rice.
Just eat the dang rice; let cauliflower be itself.
There's enough pressure to perform in the world
already.

MUCUS MINISTRY

As I wipe lotion on the inside of my four-year-old's
cracked nostrils, I feel the Spirit nudge me.
This is important, He says.
How many mothers have engaged in this mucus
ministry?
My girl says, "Thank you, Mama. You are my
best mama ever."
And I think *Yes, Lord. You are right.*
This is important.

GOVERNMENT SECRETS

I would blab any knowledge I had,
any secrets, any classified documents
of war plans, nuclear codes, secret armories,
and WMDs if it meant the writhing child in my
arms screaming terroristic threats would just
Go.
To.
Sleep.

I understand why sleep deprivation is a torture
tactic because after hours of bleary-eyed
exhaustion, I would flip on secret agents, and
tell the CIA, FBI, DEA, or ATF
anything they wanted to know if this malcontent
soldier would settle down and
Go.
To.
Sleep.

No truth serum required.

Parenthood Propaganda

Scores of people will line up to give you advice.
The messaging is clear.

To be a good mom follow this advice explicitly:

Sleep when the baby sleeps,
But wake up early for quiet time and self-care.
Self-care is important but don't be selfish.
Enjoy every minute but don't be lazy.
Babies don't keep but if your house is chaos...
Think of your mental health!
But don't go to therapy because it's not *that bad*.
You're not *actually* struggling; motherhood is just
really hard.
But it shouldn't be too hard, so if you need help
just ask.
It takes a village, but you can't depend on others to
raise your kids.
Make sure you consult the parenting books,
but don't read too much into it because we didn't
do it that way.
Don't be on your phone around your kids, but
take lots of pictures to remember them because
babies don't keep.

Play this advice on an endless loop until children
reach adulthood, then be sure to start listening to

the newest informative programming about how in spite of this indoctrination, you still somehow screwed them up.

REFINING FIRE

The refining fire of motherhood feels more like
Nebuchadnezzar's fiery furnace than the
warmth of home's hearth.
The fires of hell more than the fires of winter's
past, where we would gather together to hear old
family tales.
The fire of battle, stories told of firefights and lost
skirmishes, the landscape riddled with casualties
of the pressure of modern motherhood.

But for now the refining fire of motherhood seems
to be located behind my eyelids, or at least that's
how it feels after yet another night of up at

Twelve
One
Two
Three
Four
Five

Each time I wearily blink, I'm surprised my
eyeballs haven't become poached eggs.

So I rise again to rest in knowing that one day
the fire will burn out, and the memories will be the
coals that keep me warm in the winter.

THINGS I ASK MY CHILDREN/THINGS I ASK MYSELF

Are you drinking enough water?
Have you gone outside yet today?
Would you like a snack?
Do you need a break?
Can I hold you?
Do you know how much I love you?
Do you know how much God loves you?

MOTHERHOOD IS ART

The choreography of late nights, rocking and
swaying our kids to sleep;
The primal rhythm of labor, the guttural groans of
women throughout the ages;
The flavors swirled together over countless meals
prepared,
The songs sung over fevered heads and under
starry skies,
The stories crafted from our imagination
designed to soothe young worried minds,
All these are high and sacred art.

What is more artistic than to love from a place
that is beyond time?
What is more creative than the birth of a child?
The birth of a mother?

About to Break

the wave forms at the bottom of her ocean floor
the tension builds as it pushes flotsam and
jetsam from her mind into a swirling mass of
debris and pressure until
it forces its way to the surface where a wave of
emotion rolls forward
the froth from stress bubbling until the wave
breaks on the shore
where it rolls back into itself and
the pressure builds again
and again
and again
no beginning
no end

To the Mom on the Hard Days

To the mom on the hard days: I see you.
I see your bloodshot eyes, streaked red from
crying and puffy from no sleep.
I see your four-day-old mom bun plopped in a
ridiculous and haphazard manner on your greasy
head.
I see the yoga pants, the spit-up stains, the same
maternity shirt you wore at 8 months pregnant
and I see how even still, it looks tight.
I see how you look at your reflection and see the
stereotype of the haggard mom.

I also see the way your child's eyes light up
when they come home and see you standing in the
kitchen.
She doesn't see the greasy hair, little sister's spit
up on your yoga pants or your love handles.
She sees her mama.

And in this mirror, I see her mama too.

Idol Worship

My insecurity is an idol; I pay alms to it daily.
My thoughts always return to myself. I am more
bodily minded than heavenly-minded.
My prayers revolve around my self-obsession.

*Give me this day my daily reassurance that I am
worthy.*
Make me an instrument of my own peace.
Let my self-scrutiny be a light to my path.

But what freedom from my idols I find when I
realize that I am the only one who cares about my
dimply thighs and extra rolls.

I am the only one worshiping at my own feet.

I will not worship the false god of perfection.
I won't sacrifice my good body on the altar of
not-good enough.
I am redeemed.
My body is good because it is fearfully and
wonderfully made.
God Himself sculpted my body.
And I will treat it as such.

I Will Not Wait

I will not wait to show up in my own life because
I am afraid of jiggly arms or thunder thighs.
I will not shy from photos taken because of
tummy rolls or misplaced back fat.
I will not let a double chin keep me from laughing
until it hurts.
I will not allow vanity to shame me into missing
the gift that comes from splashing with my
children in the wild water,
Unabashed, unashamed.
Insecurity can wait, but I will not.

Fake News

Headlines and advertisements shout at me:

Try our shake!
Melt off Those Pounds!
You won't be hungry with just one little pill!
There's a skinny person just waiting inside you!
Real life waits for you on the other side of fat!

But my real life is here in this chair. Sticky cheeks
pressing against mine, tiny feet digging into
my soft stomach. There is no better life on the
other side of an arbitrary number on the scale.
This life, right here, is the best life.

I will never look as thin as I was at sixteen. That
version of me had yet to find her footing in the
world. She hadn't known the pain of birth, the joy
of her babies' first smiles, the despair of
postpartum depression, the peace in healing
through faith. Those things aren't found in
magazine articles peppered with lies and
unnecessary exclamation points.

They can't be measured on a scale or in calories
burned or consumed.

New Year's Resolutions

Will the new you be a better you?
Will the workouts you've planned create meaning
in your days?
Will the calories counted give you control over the
anxiety that plagues you?
Will you find the answers at the bottom of
your meal replacement shake?

Or will you wake up to find the curve of your
thighs pleasing to your sight?
Your diet rich with delicious food, your belly full
from a life of decadent and delightful decisions?
Will you move your body in ways that are
meaningful and loving?
Will you find that the number on the scale or the
inches of your waist do not correspond with
happiness or health?

Will your true form be seen in the eyes of an old
friend and suddenly you're a kid again at the bus
stop, your feet wet from the dew?

The totality of your worth is not found in the sum
of your gravitational pull.
Be so free from the weight of conformity that you
float above it all.

INFLUENCER

My follower count isn't very high.
The analytics can't really be measured correctly
because I'm outside of the algorithm; my influence
feels very small.
But then I see my father's eyes reflected in the
deep dark well of my daughter's irises, and my
vision clears:
My daughters pray because our petitions float over
their listening ears to God's.
The flowers bloom because I plant them.
Our garden grows because I tend it.
Our home is filled with music because we tune the
instruments and play.
We are leaving a legacy. A heritage.

I'm not building an empire; I'm cultivating a life.

To Jubilee and Rejoice and the Wild Women You Will One Day Be:

You don't have to buy the greed and discontent
that the world will try to sell you.
You don't have to answer the phone when Fear
calls to spread more doom and gloom.
You don't have to be consumed by the news.
Turn it off and love your neighbor.

You don't have to be tame.
Harness the wildness in you, guide it, like riding a
horse; the force of it carries you, but you control
the direction.
The Big Bad Wolf will come knocking on the door
ready to eat you alive, but you two wild women
will be waiting on the other side, grinning and
sharpening your knives.

There is no crystal ball; there is only God's Truth.

TRADITION

Like generations of southern mothers before me, I
march my children out front every April for the
annual photo by the azalea bush.

Each year the babies and the azaleas grow and
bloom, and I pray the roots run deep.

PANDEMIC PARENTING

Have you gone outside yet today?
Let's go outside.

Look outside
To fleabane daisies and lyre leaf sage,
To squash blossoms and tomato blooms.
To look outside of ourselves

To see a time when five pastel birthday candles
atop an apple crumb pie could feel like a miracle.

What Children Remember

We forget that death and life are separated only
by the thin veil of time.
We forget because we rush to climb up
hardscrabble mountains of our own ambition
while clinging to the hope that one day, maybe in a
few years, things will be easier.
But death is waiting.
Not in a sinister, lurking way but in a quiet
inevitable manner that is neither friendly nor
ferocious.
It only is.

But children remember what adults forget.

Their emotions are always bubbling under the
surface and explode at any inclination: tears over a
lost toy, excitement over a cool bug, joy at an
unexpected gift.
Somehow they know that every minute of this life
is a mist, and they don't hold anything back.
Quietly, the wonder and magic of childhood slips
away by degrees and is replaced with cynicism or
worse, apathy.

We are left holding an empty bag that once
contained our imagination.

Can we fill it once more?

A DOUBLE PORTION

No, I am not the first traveler to see that the
micro is actually the macro.
To see an army of myself shining in the eyes of a
grasshopper,
A cosmos in the rose petals,
To hear a symphony in the screams of the summer
cicadas,
The chorus of crickets in the tall grass.
I'm not the first, and I will not be the last.
I pray my children will pick up my mantle,
receiving a double portion of curiosity and
gratitude for this life and the One who made it.

Questions about Eternity for My Girls

Before is both a preposition and noun.
A placement of position and a place in time.
Before kids, before marriage, before school,
before the womb.
Before is where souls rest until they are tried by
fire and flesh and blood.
"Before you were formed in the womb, I knew
you." He says.

Is Eternity as long as they say?
Do you think the time of forever runs in both
directions? I do.
If our souls are eternal, were we together in the
before?
Did my soul and the two of yours know each
other?
Is that why the connection is so primal?
Because it always was and always will be?
Maybe we were tethered even then,
Separated for a while, meeting again in this
place and time.
Our souls are eternal; I pray they all meet again a
long, long time from now.

He knew you before, and so did I.

Nature at Work

I wish I were the person who always knew what
phase the moon was in,
what birds were coming home for spring,
what the tender wildflowers by the creek
answer to.
I don't know these things, but I know my babe's
cry for her mama over all the others.

That is nature at work as well.

Rejoice of Ball Ground

The light cascades over the face of the sleeping
babe in my arms.
Her eyelashes are gilded copper filaments
against her pale pink skin.
You are the stuff of poetry, I whisper.
Helen of Troy was not as beautiful as you.

Making Plans

I want my kids to have stories to tell.
Memories of red-breasted robins and chickadees,
jonquils and crocus,
pines and fiddle-head ferns.
Wild romps beneath oak trees and in creeks.
A connection to earth and the Creator.

I want more than pixels on a screen.
I want heart-racing adventure.
I want a deep connection to land and space and
water.
I want us to travel and breathe and run arms
wide open into the ocean.
I want to feel small and powerless against the infinite.

LEVIATHAN

I went to the lake today. I wanted to write outside
by the water, uninterrupted. But soon other
people's children came to show me snails they
found, and I was too distracted to write. I decided
to take a swim to a little island not far from shore.
Soon, I was in the cool deep water and the island
somehow felt farther away than before. The
freedom I felt in the water turned to fear
when I began to imagine what Leviathan
lurked just inches below my feet in the dark murky
water. I panicked and swam back to shore.

Anyway, I'm sure there's a poem in there
somewhere.

Aspirations vs. Reality

Can we stop using "aspiring" to describe our
dreams?
Either we are or we are not.
The sun isn't an aspiring light.
No, she wakes up the world every day, shining.
She just *is*.

Mothers do not aspire to mother;
They actively do the work of mothering.
Their art is one of daily practice.

Yours is too.

As the Twig is Bent So Goes the Tree

I want to bend our branches towards sunlight and
moonbeams,
Toward Truth and Grace,
Towards the Finished Work of another twig
that was bent by the Father.

Kudzu Confidence

There is no need to compare and despair.
I am a kudzu vine of blood and bone.
My roots cannot be killed by poison or spade.
I will find my way regardless of the circumstance.

Any dirt is fertile ground when you know what
you're made of.

Consistency

Consistency is key, my friend.
Look at the water, smoothing the rocks in the
creek bed.
Every day she shows up,
working.

CONSTRUCTION

Take the bricks they threw and build something
beautiful.

FAITH

It's not *just* the size of the mustard seed that
matters.
It's the surety that you plant it and it grows.
Do we forget that God will do what He says He
will do?

FEAR IS A LOUSY CONDUCTOR

What am I afraid of?
Rejection? Why?
Because if I lay bare my very soul's song, then
everyone will hear the melody.
Every harmony line, every dissonant note, and
every unexpected chord progression will be up
for the listening.

Then that song will be rejected, and all the
vulnerability of my heart's symphony will be for
nothing.

But if the cries of my heart are muted by my
pride, what is the point?
What if my song is meant for another to sing,
and they never hear it for my fear of it falling on
tone-deaf ears?
What I share is meant for others to hear; what
they do with it is a composition of their own
making.

So here is my song.
Let the band play on.

INDECISION

What do they know?
Did they knit you in your mother's womb?
Were the stars told to shine from the vibrations of
their mouth?
What does their opinion matter when the universe
bows to your Maker?
When the world revolves in His hands?

Will you let the Fear of Man keep you from your
divine purpose?
Will I?

BLESS 'EM

What does the critic have that you don't?
Too much time on their hands?
They must not have a dog that needs walking or a
garden to tend to.
A lonely existence for sure.
Do they not have mouths to feed or paint to
watch dry?
How boring their life must be to have so little
going on.
How sad!

Poor things.
Bless their heart.

ABUNDANCE

Jealousy is a scarcity mindset, and impatience is
greed.
It's all fear.
A fear that if another has what I want, there
won't be enough for me.
There is more than enough of everything to go
around.
You will not miss what is meant for you.
You will not miss what is meant for you.
You will not miss what is meant for you.
There is abundance even in the lack if you will
look for it.

Almost Famous

"Almost Famous, No Awards Yet," declared a
barbeque restaurant sign.
I appreciate the honesty and hopefulness of that
statement.
I, too, am almost famous, no awards yet.

Labor/Luck

I won't let the jealousies of others convince me I
haven't earned my spot.
I won't trade my blessings for the envy of smaller
minds.
Don't mistake my labor for luck, my friend.
I've shown up to work every day.

Manual Labor

I joked that my body was not meant for manual
labor, but look at the life I've built.

The Eighth Wonder of the World

The Great Pyramid of Giza,
The Hanging Gardens of Babylon,
The Temple of Artemis at Ephesus,
The Statue of Zeus at Olympia,
The Mausoleum at Halicarnassus
The Colossus of Rhodes,
The Lighthouse of Alexandria, and
My Reflection in the Mirror of a Dragonfly Wing

The Blood

My body knows the Truth.
The energy of the ancients course through the
umbilical cord until it's cut.
Generations of jubilation and destruction stored
within my sacred cord of DNA.
We all share the same genetic defect.
Instead of the Fates cutting the red thread,
I shed every bloody tie to the old curse and cling
to the red

rope

in

Rahab's

window.

You'll Get Lost If You Look Down

Today I went walking in our woods, but
when it came time to go home, I got lost;
The path disappeared into brambles and weeds.
The evening shadows became menacing,
and my once beloved woods became strange and
unfamiliar.

Finally, my husband and our girls came looking
for me.
My oldest daughter asked me how I got so far off
track.
I told her I was watching where I put my feet, so I
wouldn't fall.
She said, "You'll get lost if you look down,
Mama! Keep your head up!"

I want to play her tender voice on repeat in my
head.

What is Truth?

The honesty in our eldest child's eyes
The feel of your hands on me at night
The laugh from our redhead's mouth
The sound of a guitar being tuned
The harmony in my sister's throat when we sing
The sparkle of my mama's smile
The words written in red

Instagram vs. Reality

I would love to have a pristine Instagram
kitchen but the problem is we live here and my
children keep eating and
the garden keeps producing the tomatoes that are
scattered everywhere and
there are crafts to do at the counter and
coffee to drink with a friend and
noodles to make from scratch with my sister so
you see my home isn't Instagram-ready because
it's real-life ready

Who Says Being Tender is a Weakness?

Who says being tender is a weakness?
Rage is brittle, splintering into thousands of
mirrored shards.
Tenderness is wave-like, making change slow and
steady over time.
It gently laps at the sand, yet it changes shorelines
daily.
Pride is white-hot and angry, spewing hate and
spittle.
Vulnerability is the armor that protects us
From a hardened heart
A closed mind and
Empty arms.
The rage, the pride,
It's yours to swallow or choke on.
Either way you're left sputtering and gasping
on the bitter words stuck in your throat.

You've got your pride.
But what will you have left?

Where the Wildflowers Grow

My former gynecologist's office offers a procedure
called Labia Beautification, as if a woman's body is
an official government project.
Just a sad stretch of highway in need of litter
pickup and wildflowers planted.

As if my children are not wildflowers enough.

THE THINGS WE SAY INSTEAD

He stands at the door leaving for work.
We fussed and fought and tossed and turned all
night.

Feeling awkward I ask,
"What time will you be home?"
I'm sorry we fought.

"Okay, I'll see you then."
Can we be friends again?

"Be careful. I love you."
I love you. I love you.

FOR JARED

I'm here to be unreasonable.
To live a life that others don't understand.
Is it unreasonable to fill our days with each other
instead of work?
Probably.

But there are no rules, darlin'.
Ours is a love song for the long haul.

PERENNIAL BLOOMS

Somethings are dependable:
the sun,
the moon,
the daisies that bloom,
the grape-scented kudzu flowers that return year
after year with no end in sight,

And you.
Always you.

ELECTRIC

Nannie had a lamp that when you touched it, it
lit up.
I feel like that when you touch me.

TELL ME

Tell me about love.
Ours is a matter of the heart and the will.
Each day choosing each other,
Seeing each other in the faces of our children,
Searching for each other in the warmth of our bed,
Finding each other under walnut trees and full
moons.

Tell me about God and the boundlessness of His
grace.
Tell me how His love and ours was predestined
before the foundations of time,
How he handcrafted you for me and us for them,
How he made pine thickets and rhododendrons
and these two miracles.

Tell me you love me, darling.
Look at the life we've built.

GENERATIONAL WEALTH

I have doubted so many things in my life:
That the car would stop in time,
That the bills would get paid,
That the baby would *ever* stop screaming,
But I've always known that Daddy loved Mama,
and that is a gift to my children as well.

KATIE

You are a controlled burn; you know your limits.
But that doesn't mean others understand the
power of your restraint.
You are not a problem to be solved but a force
to be reckoned with;
You could warm the whole world with your flame.

Read these words again when someone tries to
quench your fire.

The Healing Power of Women

Their words are a salve, and the kind gestures a
poultice, encouraging whatever poison that is
under the surface to rise, so it can be expelled and
begin to heal.

The relationships forged through familiar fire are
reciprocal, you get what you give.
And when you can't give because life has
kicked your teeth down your throat, you mumble
through bloody lips and the healers come.

TIME KEEPERS

My life is not kept in the
days
hours
minutes
that tick by.

It's in the smell of sunscreen by the Gulf,
In the big cat-head biscuits my grandma had
waiting and the screen door slamming behind her,
the housedress she wore as she brought them to
the table on a teal melamine plate.
It's in the way the moon light drifted over my
husband under the walnut tree,
The strings on my daddy's Martin guitar,
Sam Phillips playing on the radio while digging
in the dirt with my sister,
The treasure buried in the dimples of my children.

What is the best measure of our days besides the
people we spend it with?
The only calendar I want to consult is in my laugh
lines that sparkle like spiderwebs in the dew.

They Just Know

The wildflowers stretch towards the sun even
though no one tells them what to do.
They know their purpose is praise.

Their life is worship
in submission to the one who holds the cosmos in
His hands.

What a gift to dance so easily on the breath
of God.

PATIENCE

Patience is a bulb
planted in the crisp ground
buried,
waiting
for warmth's call to burst forth
and welcome the kissing bees of spring.

DOG DAYS OF A PANDEMIC SUMMER

My husband says it's in the stars, when Sirius
rises with the sun.

I say it's when the leaves drift from the trees,
Not because it's time to fall, but because they are
just too tired to keep hanging on.

Either way, they're here.

The days stretch out parched and lonely before us.
So lonely that when the dog barks at you from
across the street,
You feel seen for the first time in weeks.
You stop in your tracks and lock eyes,
like prey and predator.

Like Orion was hunting you all along.

ORDINARY DAYS

Today I saw three bluebirds.
Three! What a marvel.
I watched as my father held my daughters'
hands and walked over a carpet of pine needles,
past a thicket of ferns,
beneath trees older than the sum of all our years.
My mother laughed, her eyes shining.
What miracles these ordinary days hold.

Ocean is Everything

Life and death wrapped up in the waves,
A soul that never stops lapping at the shore.
Ancient and powerful, she is not far away for long.
She is eternal.

For Ocean Cantley
Born September 10th, 2020.

No Logic, Only Hope

A box turtle laid her eggs in our front flower bed.
My daughter thinks it's because the mama turtle
trusts us.
How do I tell her that even we could crush them?
How do I keep her babies safe?
How do I keep *my* babies safe?
The news channels show Afghan women passing
Hope to soldiers who bear the heavy weight of a
mother's love in their arms.
My heart aches because I know Love strives to
secure the next generation.
I didn't birth my children because I thought the
world was safe for them; I loved them before I
knew them.
That's why.

There's no logic in love.
Only hope.

UNBECOMING

"That behavior is unbecoming of a lady"
Yes, it is.
I'm unbecoming what I was told I should be.

Who I am as a Christian.
What a good girl looks like.
When to speak my mind.
Where to put my energy.
How a mother conducts herself.

Unbecoming feels like a Monarch emerging from a
chrysalis, ready to migrate home.

ARSON

My faith lit the match, and the building went
up in flames.
All that is left is the smoldering structure and the
box of questions in my hand.
All that is left standing is The Truth.
Why are the questions so hard to answer?
Does the Word not say what it says?

Why do we need the trappings of religion, when
we have the God of the Universe?
If my curiosity is enough to burn it down, how
fireproof was it to start with?
The Master Builder was not in charge of that
project.
No, that was at best an apprentice, trying to
mimic The Master, but they were not as skilled as
the one who wrote the blueprints.

But when it's all burnt down, the Truth stands.
And through that Truth, so do I.
I will come out of the fire and won't even smell like
smoke.

Rest in the Waiting

Let me rest in the waiting like the deer that
pants for You.
Let me find peace while holding onto Hope.
Like the drop of dew is held in the fronds of the
fern,
Let me wait until my life is but a vapor in Your
lungs.

DEVOTION

Love waits at the garden gate.
The smell of crushed rose petals rises from the
path as she walks in the languid night.

God is a gardener, and she is made in His image.

Never presupposing, she listens to the roses
and lets them tell her what they need
Her hands tend the vines, avoiding thorns and
finding blooms.
They unfurl onto her fingers like a child
blossoming under her mother's care.
Her way seems otherworldly.

It's not magic; just attention.

Just devotion.

CICADAS

The cicadas bury themselves and emerge to shed
their hard shells once they're under the protection
of the trees.
For years they wait, hoping for a life that's safe
while preparing for danger.
If that's not prescriptive of the human condition, I
don't know what is.
Our shells are not unlike theirs, and we shed
them when we find safety.
And if we are lucky, we can climb into the trees
and scream.

Hope Is a Harp

Hope is a harp,
A megaphone,
A ballot box,
A siren's call for better days ahead.

Tiny seeds planted in preparation for juicy
tomatoes come summer.

STORIES

All of the strength of our ancestors is living inside
of us.
Their experiences culminate into ours, weaving
together like a tapestry.
Yours and mine.
Every blessing,
curse,
heartbeat,
heartbreak
brought them and me and you here.

Are we not the literal sum (and more) of their
existence?

There is more to this life than the one I've lived.
So many stories to be told by me, through me,
for me.
The stories that came before are coming
through me now.
The stories that came before are who I am now.
The stories are. And so am I.
Your story matters because it traveled through
time and blood to bear witness to its present
unfolding.

Honor its work by telling the truth.

MAKESHIFT HOSPITALITY

There's always room at my table.
Even if it wasn't built for one more, I will find
every bedside table, plant stand, or kitchen stool
to create an extension of my table for you to sit
next to me.
There's always room for one more.
Always.

God can make any old space fit for a King.

Hope Springs Eternal

Once, I had a tomato that was better than any
steak I have ever eaten.
It was a pink Brandywine and it was uglier than
homemade sin, but *just* as delicious.
I devoured it raw and covered in salt on the back
steps of a friend's house, the juice running down
my wrists.

Every tomato seed I plant, I hope it becomes that
tomato.
It has been fifteen years.
So far, no luck.
But I keep trying.

TRANSLUCENCY

We crave authenticity.
Transparency.
We look for it in little squares on our phones or
tweets on a screen.
We're hoping to find honesty.
But instead of sloppy cursive on a journal's page,
we get typed words on a screen along with a shiny
picture perfectly curated for the 'gram.

We want analog thoughts in a digital age.

Transparency is hard. We second guess all of our
thoughts before we release them to the world
because what if someone knew the real us?
We'd be rejected. Unloved. Unfollowed.

Maybe you don't feel like you can really share your
heart. You can't put it into words how you long to
feel free like you did as a kid when you would spin
around in circles so fast the world fell blurry at
your feet.
You can't describe the feeling of peace you
have when you drive with the windows down and
the sun burns your arm as you let it hang out the
window.
You're afraid to admit that once you collapsed
in the Starbucks bathroom, exhausted and afraid
someone would see you cry tears of frustration.

But people care. They want to know you. The
good, the bad, and the ugly.
So, transparency is hard.
Can we shoot for translucency?
Maybe it's the gateway to transparency.
Maybe it's a good place to start.
After all, it still lets the light in.

Am I My Brother's Keeper?

Abel's blood cried out to Him from the ground;
A life lost in anger and ignorance of God's gift.
A willful dismissal of a life made in God's image.
Millennia later, blood still cries out to Him,
poured from vessels deemed less than by hate and
evil in the hearts of men.
Still the question remains: am I my brother's
keeper?
Yes. I am.
Now what?

THE LIE

The lie bit her in the ear and laid its eggs of
unworthiness right at the opening.
When the lie hatched, it ate its way thru her ear
drum, devouring malleus, incus and stapes.
Growing plump, it found the eustachian tube, and
decided that it was hungry for more and ate her
cochlea too.
It began to burrow its way deep into the gray
matter until there was no room for anything else
but the lie.

When the bullet passed through the lie, there was
nothing left.

Just the guts of the lie and a broken heart.

I Love You

A friend once told me I saved her life by telling
her "I love you" once a week.
You don't have to say it back, but I love you.
The world needs you.
This is your sign to stay.

MANTRAS

My body is a temple.
My scars are beautiful.
My broken heart is worth mending.
If I repeat it enough, it must be true.

I Guess I'll Try to Hurry Up?

"When will you get over it?"

Tell me, what is the time table for getting over a
broken heart?
Give me a month to catch my breath, at least.
Can I have three months to finish crying?
Is six months long enough for the gaping hole
in my chest to scab over and close?
Let me know when you think I've grieved enough.

Maybe the bruises will be yellow-green and gone
by then.

SOCIAL SECURITY

You did me a kindness by leaving.
I didn't see it that way at the time, of course;

A child doesn't understand why she can't play
with fire.

You went your way and I went mine.
I wish you well.
But it still stings when I think of how our laughter
was carried away on the breeze.
Don't worry, your secrets are still safe with me.

A Poem of Minor Inconveniences

Since seeing your comments online about your
wife, I can only assume that you must be an idiot.
To not appreciate such a quality person must be
proof positive of your lack of intelligence.
So, to celebrate this unadulterated idiocy, I hope
the universe rewards you with a series of
minor inconveniences such as these until you come
to your senses:

Waking up and stepping in cat puke,
Catching every single red light when you're in a
hurry or
An error message every time you try to print
something.
Maybe you'll clog a toilet at your boss's house or
Get caught picking your nose in traffic.
If your pinkie toe finds every chair leg or
A wispy cat hair sticks in your eyelashes so that it
scrapes your eye all day with no relief,
That will be fine with me.

An itch you can't scratch, a need you can't meet, a
desire just out of reach.

May you always have an unexpected item in the
bagging area until you realize
the woman you mocked,
the woman you married,

86

the woman who bore your child,
the woman who *chose* you
deserves more than the jokes you share online
at her expense.

Is she nothing more than a minor inconvenience
to you?
Or is she your wife?

Home Sweet Home

Church isn't meant to be silent, a library full of
saints.
Was there ever a happy home that was quiet?

It's a kitchen table where you pull out a chair
and ask your questions,
A place to cry in anger, a place to ask your dad to
fix what hurts.
A place to plant hope and watch it flower and
when it wilts, wait for spring again.
A place to run wild with abandon until you fall
asleep talking to the Father.

DEATH

Death comes as an unexpected dinner guest.
He barges in uninvited and begins to wreak his
havoc over the supper table, scattering crumbs and
candle wax all over our fine tablecloth.
He wastes our time with talk of angry politics
and ugly religion.
But what is time to a thief?
He slowly empties our table until the chairs
here sit lonely, and somewhere far away there is
laughter once more.
He leaves what is left on his plate and takes his exit.

Rude.

But one day, dead bones will rise.
Death will not come calling again,
And the one who holds the keys will wipe away all
tears.

God will wipe away every tear from their eyes; and
death shall be no more...

And Yet

The world is so loud.
Voices yelling, stampeding over one another.
Poised to react, not respond.
And yet, rising above the din
There's a still, small voice.

If only we would listen.

LOST AT SEA

I am a ship lost at sea.
The waves rock and smash over my bow,
leaving me vulnerable and exposed to the bitter salt
of the water.
What I forget is that my ship is actually in a bottle
of my own tears that the psalms say You save.
When the saltiness of the waves rolls down my
face, I am held in the hands of the shipbuilder.
Even if I shipwreck, it will be against the Rock of
Ages.

You are the only one who can calm the waves.
Peace, be still.

NAKED

Naked on the beach, I stand with the Gulf's waves
lapping at my feet. Free. My friends stand
behind me wearing both clothes and looks of
shock on their faces. The salt and wind always
coax the wild in me, but this is the first time I act
without thinking and do what I always *want* to do:
somehow slide back into the warm primordial wet
that we all come from, no separation between the
Created and the Creator. The breeze whips my
hair loose from its bun and, turning to untangle it
from my eyelashes, I see my sisterhood of friends
behind me. They're laughing and making plans to
be so bold tomorrow night when it's a little darker
and they have sufficiently convinced each other to
be so wild. They make plans; I revel in the now.

When we walk back, I shove my bra into my back
pocket, and I wrap this moment up to look at
later.

The next night, we walk on the beach together
until after dark. We walk past all the fishermen and
the families with flashlights looking for ghost crabs
that scuttle along the water's edge. We walk until
the lights and people are nothing more than hints
of shadows, and then we walk some more just to
be safe. We all giggle while we strip down to our
most basic selves, our bodies bare, and we laugh at

what our husbands and boyfriends will say when
we tell them about our adventure. Our bodies are
different shapes and sizes, sun-kissed and stretched
from athletics and babies, all freckled curves and
soft secrets. We set up a camera on a self-timer to
take a group shot of our backs while we face the
vast dark water lit by moonlight. We each get a
Polaroid of the shot, and we look like we could be
in a postcard. In that one moment of primal
innocence, we are not wives or mothers or both;
we are women left free and small on the edge of
forever.

My eternal soul breathes.

ACKNOWLEDGMENTS

I'd like to thank so many people for the wonderful gift of their time and energy, for pouring so much into my life that my cup runs over. I've started writing this page so many times, and I cannot find the right words to explain how blessed I have been to have so many wonderful and uplifting people in my corner. So, to start:

Jared: There aren't words enough to tell you how your sacrificial love has shaped my life into what it is today. Besides salvation, you are my greatest gift. I've loved you since I was seventeen, and I will love you forever.

Jubilee and Rejoice: You girls are the stuff dreams are made of. The Lord gave me the desires of my heart when He gave y'all to me. I love you both so much!

Mama and Daddy: What a blessing to have been raised by such loving and weird people. I saw love in action every day and that will be y'all's legacy for generations to come. Thank you for loving me and showing me Jesus.

Katie and Asa: I hope you know how much I love you. I am so unbelievably proud of you both for what you've allowed God to do in your lives. Katie, you are the reason I wanted to have two girls, so that mine would have with each other what I have with you. I will be your go-to ugly girl forever!

Ma and Pops: It is a gift to have in-laws like y'all! I wish everyone could experience the kind of love from their in-laws that I feel from you two. I literally could not parent without y'all. You help me be a better mama. I've never felt like I wasn't part of the family, and I've always appreciated that.

Ian: I will cry if I start explaining what I feel when I look at you. You are a testament to God's divine grace and I love you so much. That's all I can say because now I need tissues.

To my sweet friends Sharee, Kelsey, Vicky, Jenny, Ashley D, Susanna, Terra, Ashley C, Kristen, Cat, Jess, Kim, and Tori: I am humbled by y'all's friendships. The love y'all show me on a daily basis is more than some could hope for in a lifetime. I am forever grateful to God for allowing me to be a part of y'all's lives and for the glorious invention of the internet that makes it possible. "The Healing Power of Women" is about y'all.

Special thanks to Cat Queen and her editing skills and fellow author Stephanie Dunham for her unending patience with all my questions about publishing. She formatted this book for publication! Without these two, this book may not have made it into the world.

There are so many other friends and family to include here, but there is no way that I could mention them all. Just know that if you're reading this, you have a special spot in my heart and I am grateful that you are here. I love you. I love y'all so much!

About the Author

Tristan Tuttle is a writer and poet who lives in north Georgia with her husband Jared and their two daughters, Jubilee and Rejoice. She spends her days chasing her girls through the garden rows and writing about it. Her poems are often found at the intersection of motherhood, nature, and spirituality, and for an added layer of vulnerability, she often makes videos and voice overs of her poetry. She can be found on www.tristantuttle.com as well as on instagram @tristantuttle and under the hashtag #tristantuttlewrites.

CPSIA information can be obtained
at www.ICGtesting.com
Printed in the USA
LVHW080001110422
715852LV00009B/413